Smoothie For Beginners

1000 Days Smoothies Recipes to Lose Weight, Gain Energy, Fight Disease, Detox and Live Long. Bonus Crash Course to Make Tasty Smoothie

DENISE ROGERS

© **Copyright 2022 by Denise Rogers - All rights reserved**.

This document is geared towards providing exact and reliable information in regard to the topic and issue covered.

- From a Declaration of Principles which was accepted and approved equally by a Committee of the American Bar Association and a Committee of Publishers and Associations.

In no way is it legal to reproduce, duplicate, or transmit any part of this document in either electronic means or in printed format. All rights reserved.

The information provided herein is stated to be truthful and consistent, in that any liability, in terms of inattention or otherwise, by any usage or abuse of any policies, processes, or directions contained within is the solitary and utter responsibility of the recipient reader.

Under no circumstances will any legal responsibility or blame be held against the publisher for any reparation, damages, or monetary loss due to the information herein, either directly or indirectly.
Respective authors own all copyrights not held by the publisher.

The information herein is offered for informational purposes solely and is universal as so. The presentation of the information is without contract or any type of guarantee assurance.

The trademarks that are used are without any consent, and the publication of the trademark is without permission or backing by the trademark owner. All trademarks and brands within this book are for clarifying purposes only and are owned by the owners themselves, not affiliated with this document.

Copyrights

This document is geared towards providing exact and reliable information regarding the topic and issue covered.

- From a Declaration of Principles which was accepted and approved equally by a Committee of the American Bar Association and a Committee of Publishers and Associations.

In no way is it legal to reproduce, duplicate, or transmit any part of this document in either electronic means or printed format. All rights reserved.

The information provided herein is stated to be truthful and consistent in that any liability, in terms of inattention or otherwise, by any usage or abuse of any policies, processes, or directions contained within is the solitary and utter responsibility of the recipient reader.

Under no circumstances will any legal responsibility or blame be held against the publisher for any reparation, damages, or monetary loss due to the information herein, either directly or indirectly.

Respective authors own all copyrights not held by the publisher.

The information herein is solely offered for informational purposes and is universal. The presentation of the information is without a contract or any guarantee assurance.

The trademarks used are without any consent, and the trademark publication is without permission or backing by the trademark owner. All trademarks and brands within this book are for clarifying purposes only and are owned by the owners, not affiliated with this document.

Smoothie

TABLE OF CONTENTS

SMOOTHIE BASICS 5
   WHAT IS THE WORD "SMOOTHIE? 5
   SMOOTHIE Vs. JUICE 5
   THE ADVANTAGES OF SMOOTHIES AND JUICE 7

MAKING YOUR SMOOTHIE 8
   BASES TO HELP YOU SMOOTHIE 8
   PRODUCTION PROCEDURE 9
   SMOOTHIE PRECAUTIONS 10

BREAKFAST SMOOTHIE 13
   Berry Banana Smoothie 13
   Mango Peach Smoothie 14
   Peanut butter and chocolate smoothie 15
   Green Machine Smoothie 16
   Pineapple Coconut Smoothie 17
   Chocolate Strawberry Smoothie 18
   Apple Pie Smoothie 19
   Chocolate Banana Smoothie 20
   Cacao and the Coffee Smoothie 21
   Pina Colada Smoothie 22
   Banana and chocolate chip smoothie 23
   Cranberries and Orange Smoothie 24
   The mint and watermelon smoothie 25
   Ginger and carrot smoothie 26
   Strawberry Oat smoothie 27

ENERGY SMOOTHIE 28
   Banana Oat Smoothie 28
   Chocolate Protein Smoothie 29
   Blueberry as well as Spinach Smoothie 30
   Strawberry with the Almond Butter Smoothie 31
   Mango along with Chia Seed Smoothie 32
   Green Energy Smoothie 33
   Cacao as well as Maca Smoothie 34
   Beets and Berries Smoothie 35
   Turmeric as well as Ginger Smoothie 36

- Power Boosting Smoothie 37
- Apple Pie Smoothie 38
- Avocado and Lime smoothie 39
- Chocolate with a Coconut smoothie 40
- Cocoa and Peanut Butter Smoothie 41
- Coconut as well as Banana Smoothie 42

MEAL-REPLENISHMENT SMOOTHIE 43

- Chocolate Peanut Butter Protein Smoothie 43
- Green Protein Smoothie 44
- Fruit Protein Smoothie 45
- A Banana and Oat Smoothie 46
- The Chocolate-covered Strawberry Smoothie 47
- Superfood Smoothie 48
- Avocado and Mango Smoothie 49
- Chocolate Banana Protein Smoothie 50
- Spinach with Banana Protein Smoothie 51
- Carrot as well as orange Protein Smoothie 52
- Peanut Butter and Banana Smoothie 53
- Strawberry as well as Oat Smoothie 54
- Blueberry with Greek Yogurt Smoothie 55
- Chocolate, as well as the Almond Butter Smoothie 56
- Pineapple as well as Coconut Smoothie 57

DETOXIFYING AND CLEANSING SMOOTHIE 58

- Green Detox Smoothie 58
- Lemon and Ginger Smoothie 59
- Beet as well as Berry Cleansing Smoothie 60
- Apple Detox and Cabbage Smoothie 61
- Ginger as well as Turmeric Smoothie 62
- Cilantro with Lemon Detox Smoothie 63
- Culver and celery Smoothie to Detox 64
- Beet as well as Carrot Detox Smoothie 65
- Spinach along with Kale Detox Smoothie 66
- Lemon and ginger Smoothie for Detox 67
- Cucumber and Mint Detox Smoothie 68
- Chia as well as Flaxseed Detox Smoothie 69

Avocado as well as Banana Smoothie to detox 70

Turmeric and ginger Detox Smoothie 71

Lemon and Ginger Smoothie 72

VEGETABLE AND VEGAN SMOOTHIES 74

Green Goddess Smoothie 74

Carrot as well as Ginger Smoothie 75

Sweet Potato Smoothie 76

Cucumber as well as Mint Smoothie 77

Broccoli along with Apple Smoothie 78

Beet as well as Berry Smoothie 79

Kale along with Apple Smoothie 80

The Banana Squash Smoothie and the Squash 81

Spinach and Cucumber Smoothie 82

Carrot as well as Ginger Smoothie 83

Cauliflower along with Banana Smoothie 84

Kale along with Pineapple Smoothie 85

Broccoli along with Apple Smoothie 86

Mango and Squash Smoothies 87

Spinach as well as Avocado Smoothie 88

ANTI-AGING SMOOTHIES 89

Blueberry as well as Acai Smoothie 89

The Pomegranate, Green Tea Smoothie 90

Strawberry as well as Kale Smoothie 91

Papaya as well as Pineapple Smoothie 92

Avocado as well as Spinach Smoothie 93

Turmeric as well as Ginger Smoothie 94

Blueberry as well as Kale Smoothie 95

Pomegranate and Flaxseed Smoothie 96

Goji Berries along with Almond Smoothie 97

Acai along with Strawberry Smoothie 98

Chia, along with Raspberry Smoothie 99

Turmeric as well as Pineapple Smoothie 100

Beet with Blueberry Smoothie 101

Spinach as well as Kale Smoothie 102

Green Tea and Avocado Smoothie 103

BUBBLE TEA RECIPES 105
Tea Strawberry bubble 105
Mango champagne tea 106
Pineapple bubble tea 107
Blueberry Bubble tea 108
Mango Blend of bubble tea 109
Strawberry Bubble Tea Smoothie 110
Pineapple bubble tea smoothie 111
Tea Peach Bubble 112
Pineapple Coconut Bubble tea 113
Mango champagne tea 114
CONCLUSION 115
MEASUREMENT CONVERSION TABLE 116

SMOOTHIE BASICS

The world is yours to discover! This book will look into the healthy and delicious world of blended fruit and vegetables. Smoothies are a fast and easy method of increasing nutrients and energy, and they're ideal for busy people who are always on the move. If you're a beginner in smoothies or an experienced professional, there are numerous new and intriguing recipes to experiment with. In this chapter, we'll discuss the fundamentals of a smoothie, including its ingredients and nutritional advantages. So, grab your blender, and let's get going!

WHAT IS THE WORD "SMOOTHIE?

The smoothie can be described as a well-known mixed drink that usually comprises ice, fruit, and a liquid base like yogurt, juice, or milk. The ingredients are blended until they are smooth and creamy, creating a refreshing and healthy drink.

Smoothies are a fantastic method of getting an amount of fruit and other nutrients in an easy and tasty form. They can be made to meet your individual preferences and dietary requirements and include options to add proteins, fiber, and other nutritious ingredients.

Smoothies are great as breakfast alternatives, a pick-me-up mid-day, or even an afternoon treat. They are also excellent for using fresh fruits and vegetables before they turn bad.

Making your smoothie is simple and affordable. Add your preferred ingredients to a blender, and mix until smooth. You can also play around with various flavor combinations to discover the perfect recipe.

Overall, smoothies are flexible, healthy, and delicious options that can be enjoyed at any time of the day.

SMOOTHIE Vs. JUICE

Smoothies and juices are two of the most popular options in healthy drinks. But, there are essential differences between them that could make one the better choice for you based on your preferences and needs.

Juice is produced by removing the liquid from vegetables and fruits and removing some fiber and pulp. It is a beverage packed with minerals and vitamins, and sugar. Juices are also deficient in the fiber found in the whole fruit and vegetable, which can slow the absorption process of sugar and keep you feeling full.

Smoothies, On the other hand, can be made by mixing whole vegetables and fruits, including their pulp and fiber. That means smoothies are an excellent source of nutrients, as they contain all the minerals, vitamins, and fiber found in veggies and fruits. In addition, the fiber content in smoothies could help slow sugar absorption and help you feel fuller for longer.

A further difference between them can be seen in how they are made. Juice tends to be smoother than smoothies. They are dense because of the presence of fiber and pulp.

In conclusion, both juices and smoothies can indeed be healthy alternatives. However, smoothies are considered a greater source of nutrients since they contain fiber and pulp found in vegetables and fruits. Additionally, they are more filling, making them an excellent option for those seeking food replacement. But, it can be an ideal choice to pursue a low-calorie and lower-volume drink that still supplies people with some of the vitamins and minerals found in fruits and vegetables.

SCAN ME

THE ADVANTAGES OF SMOOTHIES AND JUICE

Smoothies and juices are healthy and delicious alternatives for those who want to improve their energy and health. Both are made with fresh vegetables and fruits and have many benefits for those who drink these drinks.

The benefits of smoothies and juices include:

- A high nutrient content Smoothies and juices are packed with vitamins, antioxidants, and minerals crucial to maintaining good health. Both vegetables and fruits are high in fiber, essential to maintaining an optimal digestive system.
- Energy levels are increased: The natural sugars found in fruit and vegetables can provide an instant energy boost, making juices and smoothies an excellent choice for people seeking to boost their energy levels.
- Aids in weight loss Smoothies and juices can be low in calories and high in nutrients, making them an ideal choice for those trying to shed weight. They can also lessen the cravings for unhealthy food.
- Improves digestion: The fiber content in vegetables and fruits can assist in improving digestion and keep your gut healthy and healthy.
- It helps to cleanse the body Smoothies and juices can help flush out impurities and toxins in the body, improving overall health and wellbeing.
- Many options for smoothies and juices can be made using various fruits and vegetables, allowing you to taste multiple flavor profiles and health advantages.
- Simple and quick to make Smoothies and juices are made quickly and quickly and are an excellent choice for busy people who are always on the move.
- Multi-purpose: Juice can serve as a stand-alone beverage, while smoothies can be utilized as a meal replacement or as an addition to an existing meal.

Juice and smoothies are delicious and nutritious options that provide various health advantages. Integrating them into your daily routine will boost your health and wellbeing quality.

MAKING YOUR SMOOTHIE

Making your smoothies at home is a great and simple way to get the advantages of fresh fruits and veggies in a tasty and practical format. This section will cover all you should learn about making your drinks, including the fundamentals of ingredients, equipment, techniques, and ingredients. Whether you're a beginner or a pro at it, there are many new and exciting concepts to explore.

The first step is the fundamentals of choosing the best ingredient, such as selecting the most suitable vegetables and fruits and the most effective ways to prepare the ingredients. We'll also discuss the various equipment needed to prepare smoothies, starting with basic blenders to top-of-the-line models. We'll also discuss different methods for mixing, blending as well as garnishing smoothies to ensure the most flavor and nutrients.

With the knowledge and tricks provided in this chapter, you'll be well on the path to creating delicious and nutritious smoothies your loved ones will surely enjoy. Get ready to wear your apron, get your blender out and get to work!

BASES TO HELP YOU SMOOTHIE

When making smoothies, there are a variety of bases to make delicious and healthy blends. Below are five easy-to-find smoothie bases that can be used to make many different smoothie recipes:

- Greek yogurt: Greek yogurt makes a rich and creamy smoothie base that keeps you feeling full and content. It's great with bananas, berries, and tropical fruits.
- Milk: Milk is a traditional base for smoothies that are high in calcium and other vital nutrients. It is creamy in texture that is great with fruits such as bananas, berries, and chocolate.
- Almond milk: It is a dairy-free smoothie base that is rich in healthy fats and low in calories. It is nutty in flavor and goes well with other fruits such as bananas, berries, and tropical fruit.
- Coconut milk: Coconut milk is a smooth and delicious base for smoothies rich in healthy fats. It adds a tropical flavor to the drink. It's great with fruit like mango, pineapple, and fruits.

- Avocado: Avocado is a rich and creamy smoothie base rich in fiber and healthy fats. It provides a smooth and soft texture to your smoothie. It is an excellent match for bananas, berries, and tropical fruits.

PRODUCTION PROCEDURE

- Making smoothies is an easy and simple procedure that can be accomplished in just a few simple steps. Here's a general guideline for creating the perfect smoothie:

- Make sure you have all the ingredients ready: before you start, ensure you have everything you require for your smoothie. This includes the choice of fruits and veggies and any additional ingredients, such as milk, yogurt, or honey.

- Get your ingredients ready. Clean and cut your vegetables and fruits into small pieces that can be mixed easily. If you're using frozen fruit, there is no need to defrost them.

- Include liquids: add the beverage of your choice on a liquid basis to the blender. It could be yogurt, milk juice, juice, or even water. The quantity of liquid used will be determined by the consistency you like. A good rule of thumb is to begin at a low amount and then increase it as you need.

- Add the fruits and veggies. Mix the prepared fruits and veggies in the blender. Begin by adding the soft vegetable and fruits before adding the more abrasive ones later.

- Blend: Put the lid onto your blender, and mix the contents at an extremely low speed for around 10 seconds. After that, increase the speed and blend for 30 seconds or so until all the ingredients have been blended.

- Adjust the consistency. The smoothie should be adjusted to suit your needs. If it is too thick, you can add more liquid, then blend again. If it's too thin, add additional fruits and vegetables, then blend again.

- Serve When the smoothie is entirely smooth and is what you like Pour the drink into glasses and drink it up.

- Add-ons: You could add various toppings to your smoothie, such as seeds, nuts, protein powder, and chocolate chips.

- Be sure that you clean your blender thoroughly after each use.

- If you follow these easy steps, you can make healthy and delicious smoothies customized to your tastes. After a few times, you'll be able to play around with various ingredients and make your smoothie recipes.

SMOOTHIE PRECAUTIONS

Smoothies can be tasty and healthy additions to your diet; however, there are some steps you need to take before making and drinking smoothies. Here are some essential tips to remember when making smoothies and drinking them:

- Take note of the size of your portions The smoothies you consume can be very packed with calories and sugar, So it's vital to be aware of portions. Begin with a small glass (about 8-12 12 ounces), and then increase the amount as you need.

- Be cautious with the sweeteners that are added. Some commercial smoothies are made with added sugars, making it essential to be aware of how much sweetener including in smoothies. To add sweetness to your smoothie, you can use natural sweeteners like maple syrup or honey.

- Be aware of fruits that are high in natural sugars. Certain fruits such as mango, pineapple, bananas, and pineapple contain a lot of natural sugars. So be aware of the amount of these fruits you include in your smoothie.

- Take note of any food sensitivities. Be aware of sensitivities or allergies to food when making smoothies. If you are allergic to nuts, make sure not to use dairy products or nut butter in your smoothies.

- Blend safely: Always be sure you properly clean your blender after using it to avoid cross-contamination between ingredients.

- Drink them immediately after preparation Smoothies are best eaten soon after making them since they diminish their nutritional value in time.

- Avoid over-blending. Over-blending could cause the ingredients to become hot and cause the destruction of some enzymes and vitamins in the vegetables and fruits.

If you follow these guidelines by following them, you can be sure that the smoothies you make are as nutritious and nutritious as they can be and still taste tasty. Smoothies are an excellent method to increase your nutritional intake, but you need to pay attention to what ingredients are used and the amount of food you consume.

The following chapter covered the fundamentals of creating homemade smoothies, including the importance of selecting the right ingredients, equipment, and techniques. We also addressed the steps to take when making and eating smoothies. Once you've got an excellent knowledge of preparing smoothies at home, you're ready to put your knowledge into action.

In the next chapter of this guide, you'll discover an array of delicious and nutritious smoothie recipes you can prepare at home. These recipes are made to meet a range of tastes, from fruity and sweet to healthy and green. Recipes are included that are breakfast-style smoothies, post-workout smoothies as well as smoothies to serve as desserts.

We invite you to play with different flavors and ingredient combinations to make smoothie recipes. Be aware that making a smoothie isn't an exact science, and you can alter the quantity and ingredients according to your preferences.

So, get your blender and prepare to experiment with tasty and nutritious smoothie recipes. Enjoy your smoothies!

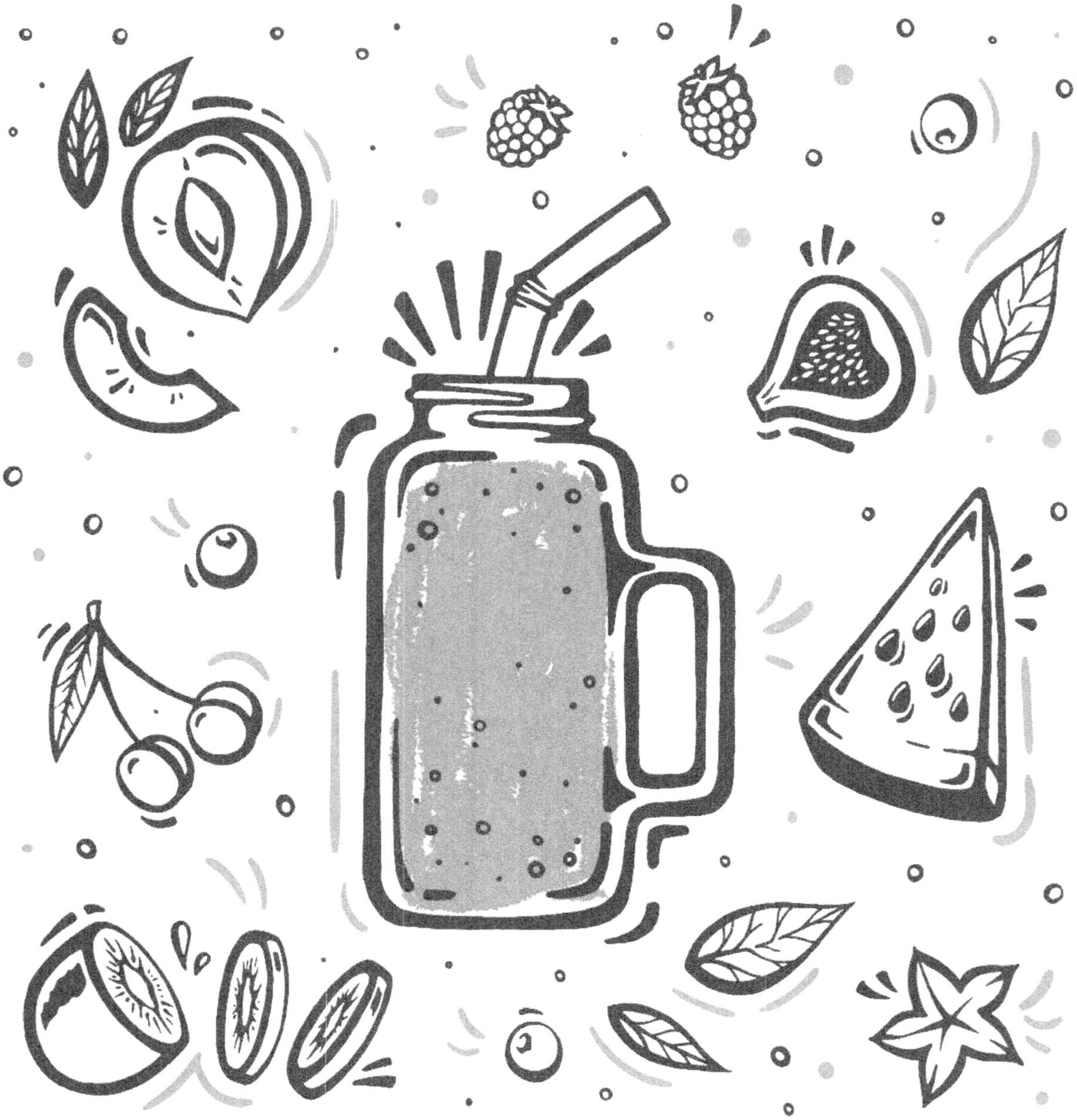

BREAKFAST SMOOTHIE
Berry Banana Smoothie

This classic smoothie is delicious and a healthy way to kick off your day. The smooth banana can perfectly balance out the berry's sweetness.

Ingredients:

- 1 banana, cut and frozen
- 1 cup frozen berries (strawberries, blueberries, raspberries)
- 1/2 cup plain Greek yogurt
- 1/2 cup almond or milk milk
- 1 tablespoon honey

Preparation:

- Blend in a food processor, and mix the berries, bananas, yogurt, milk, and honey.
- Blend at a highly high-speed setting until the blend is uniform. It should take about 30 minutes.
- If your smoothie seems too thick, pour the milk and blend it again.
- Pour it into a glass, and sip.

Mango Peach Smoothie

This refreshing tropical drink will take the tastebuds to a cozy and sunny spot. The combination of peach and mango provides a delicious and sweet flavor.

Ingredients:

- 1 ripe peach pitted and cut into pieces
- 1 mango ripe Peeled and cut into dice
- 1 banana, cut into slices
- 1 cup of orange juice
- 1/2 cup Greek yogurt
- 1/4 cup of ice

Preparation:

- Blend the mango, peach orange juice, banana, Greek yogurt, and ice with a mixer.
- Blend at the highest speed to blend until it is smooth. It should take about 30 minutes.
- If the drink is thick enough, you can add orange juice and blend it again.
- Pour it into a glass, and then sip.

Peanut butter and chocolate smoothie

A healthy and delicious way of satisfying sweet tooth cravings, This smoothie is loaded with nutrients and healthy fats.

Ingredients:

- 1 banana, cut into slices
- 1/2 cup plain Greek yogurt
- 1/2 cup of almond milk or milk
- 2 tablespoons of unsweetened cocoa powder
- 2.25 tablespoons peanut butter
- 1 tablespoon honey

Preparation:

- Blend in a food processor, mix the yogurt, banana, cocoa powder, honey, peanut butter, and.
- Blend at a highly high-speed setting until the blend is uniform. It should take about 30 minutes.
- If the mixture is thicker, you can add milk and blend it.
- Pour it into a glass, and sip.

Green Machine Smoothie

This smoothie is loaded with leafy greens and is an ideal method to receive your regular intake of minerals and vitamins.

Ingredients:

- 1 banana, cut into slices
- 1/2 cup frozen pineapple
- 1/2 cup baby spinach
- 1/2 cup Greek yogurt
- Half a cup of coconut water
- 1 tablespoon honey

Preparation:

- Blend in a food processor and blend the pineapple, banana, spinach, coconut water, yogurt, and honey.
- Blend at the highest speed to blend until it is smooth, approximately 30 minutes.
- If your smoothie seems too thick, mix in coconut water and blend again.
- Pour it into a glass, and sip.

Pineapple Coconut Smoothie

This smoothie is the perfect mix of tropical tastes that transport your preferences to a tropical island.

Ingredients:

- 1 cup frozen pineapple
- 1/2 cup coconut milk
- 1/2 cup Greek yogurt
- 1/4 cup of ice
- 1 tablespoon honey

Preparation:

- Blend in a food processor, and blend the coconut milk, pineapple, Greek yogurt, ice, and honey.
- Blend at high speed until it is smooth—approximately 30 seconds.
- If your smoothie seems too thick, mix in coconut water and blend it again.
- Pour it into a glass, and then sip.

Chocolate Strawberry Smoothie

A healthy and delicious breakfast to kick off your day This smoothie is brimming in antioxidants, healthy fats, and antioxidants.

Ingredients:

- 1 Cup frozen strawberry
- 1 banana, cut into slices
- 1/2 cup plain Greek yogurt
- 1/2 cup of almond milk or milk
- 2 tablespoons of unsweetened cocoa powder
- 1 tablespoon honey

Preparation:

- Blender: mix the banana, strawberries, milk, yogurt, cocoa powder, and honey.
- Blend at the highest speed to blend until it is smooth. It should take about 30 minutes.
- If the mixture is thicker, you can add milk and blend it.
- Pour the drink into a glass and then sip.

Apple Pie Smoothie

This smoothie is a delicious, nutritious way to indulge in the apple pie's flavors without guilt.

Ingredients:

- 1 apple Cored, peeled and peeled
- 1 banana, cut into slices
- 1/2 cup plain Greek yogurt
- 1/2 cup almond or milk milk
- 1 teaspoon of ground cinnamon
- 1 tablespoon honey

Preparation:

- Blend in a blender. Blend the banana, apple milk, yogurt, cinnamon, and honey.
- Blend at a highly high-speed setting until the blend is uniform. It should take about 30 minutes.
- If the mixture is thicker, you can add milk and blend it.
- Pour it into a glass, and then sip.

Chocolate Banana Smoothie

This smoothie is a healthy and delicious breakfast option with antioxidants and potassium.

Ingredients:

- 1 banana, cut into slices
- 1/2 cup plain Greek yogurt
- 1/2 cup almond or milk milk
- 2 tablespoons of unsweetened cocoa powder
- 1 tablespoon honey

Preparation:

- Mix the banana, yogurt, cocoa powder, and honey with a blender.
- Blend at a highly high-speed setting until the blend is uniform, approximately 30 minutes.
- If your smoothie seems too thick, pour the milk and blend it again.
- Pour the drink into a glass and then sip.

Cacao and the Coffee Smoothie

This smoothie is a deliciously nutritious way to begin your day. It will give you an extra energy boost due to the caffeine in the coffee and the cacao antioxidants.

Ingredients:

- 1 banana, cut into slices
- 1/2 cup plain Greek yogurt
- 1/2 cup of almond milk or milk
- 2 tablespoons of unsweetened cacao powder
- 1 shot of espresso or 1/2 cup of strong, strong-brewed coffee
- 1 tablespoon honey

Preparation:

- Blender: mix the yogurt, banana, and milk with coffee powder, cacao powder, and honey.
- Blend at the highest speed to blend until it is smooth, approximately 30 minutes.
- If your smoothie seems too thick, pour the milk and blend it again.
- Pour it into a glass, and sip.

Pina Colada Smoothie

This smoothie is a tasty, nutritious way to kick off the day with an exotic flair.

Ingredients:

- 1 cup frozen pineapple
- 1/2 cup coconut milk
- 1/2 cup Greek yogurt
- 1/4 cup of ice
- 1 tablespoon honey
- 1/4 teaspoon vanilla extract

Preparation:

- Blend in a food processor, blend the coconut milk, pineapple, Greek yogurt, ice, honey, and vanilla extract.
- Blend at a highly high-speed setting until the blend is uniform, approximately 30 minutes.
- If the drink is thick enough, you can add more coconut milk and blend again.
- Pour it into a glass, and sip.

Banana and chocolate chip smoothie

Delicious and healthy breakfast option This smoothie is brimming with antioxidants and potassium.

Ingredients:

- 1 banana, cut into slices
- 1/2 cup plain Greek yogurt
- 1/2 cup almond or milk milk
- 1 teaspoon chocolate chips
- 1 tablespoon honey

Preparation:

- Mix the yogurt, banana, chocolate chips, milk, and honey in a food processor.
- Blend at a highly high-speed setting until the blend is uniform, approximately 30 minutes.
- If your smoothie seems too thick, pour the milk and blend it again.
- Pour the drink into a glass and sip.

Cranberries and Orange Smoothie

This smoothie is a delicious and healthy method to kick off your day. It will give you an extra dose of Vitamin C thanks to the citrus and the cranberries.

Ingredients:

- 1 cup cranberries
- 1 cup of orange juice
- 1/2 cup Greek yogurt
- 1/4 cup of ice
- 1 tablespoon honey

Preparation:

- Mix the fruits, orange juice, Greek yogurt, ice, and honey with a blender.
- Blend at the highest speed to blend until it is smooth. It should take about 30 minutes.
- If the drink is thick enough, you can add orange juice and blend it again.
- Pour the drink into a glass and then sip.

The mint and watermelon smoothie

This smoothie is a healthy and delicious way to begin your day. It will help you feel refreshed by the mint and watermelon.

Ingredients:

- 2 cups watermelon seedless cubed
- 1/2 cup plain Greek yogurt
- 1/2 cup of almond milk or milk
- 1 tablespoon honey
- 5-6 mint leaves

Preparation:

- With a blender, blend the yogurt, watermelon, honey, milk, and mint leaves.
- Blend at the highest speed to blend until it is smooth, approximately 30 minutes.
- If your smoothie seems too thick, pour the milk and blend it again.
- Pour it into a glass, and then sip.

Ginger and carrot smoothie

This smoothie is a tasty, nutritious way to kick off your day. It is loaded with antioxidants and vitamins.

Ingredients:

- 1 cup of grated carrots
- 1 cup of orange juice
- 1/2 cup Greek yogurt
- 1/8-inch pieces of ginger
- 1 tablespoon honey

Preparation:

- Mix the juice of oranges, carrots, Greek yogurt, ginger, and honey with a blender.
- Blend at a highly high-speed setting until the blend is uniform, approximately 30 minutes.
- If the drink is thick enough, you can add orange juice and blend it again.
- Pour the drink into a glass and then sip.

Strawberry Oat smoothie

This smoothie is a tasty, nutritious way to kick off your day. It's full of antioxidants and fiber.

Ingredients:

- 1 cup of frozen strawberries
- 1/2 cup plain Greek yogurt
- 1/2 cup of almond milk or milk
- 1/4 cup of rolled oats
- 1 tablespoon honey

Preparation:

- With a blender, mix the yogurt, strawberries, milk, oats, and honey.
- Blend at the highest speed to blend until it is smooth. It should take about 30 minutes.
- If the mixture is thicker, you can add milk and blend it.
- Pour the drink into a glass and sip.

ENERGY SMOOTHIE
Banana Oat Smoothie

This smoothie is an excellent way to begin your day or for a quick boost during the afternoon. Oats will supply you with energy for the long haul, and the banana will give you an immediate energy boost.

Ingredients:

- 1 banana
- 1/2 cup of rolled oats
- 1/2 cup Greek yogurt
- 1/2 cup almond or milk milk
- 1 tablespoon honey
- 1/4 teaspoon vanilla extract

Preparation:

- Blend in a food processor, and mix the banana, oatmeal milk, yogurt, honey, and vanilla extract.
- Blend at the highest speed to blend until it is smooth. It should take about 30 minutes.
- If the mixture is thicker, you can add milk and blend it.
- Pour the drink into a glass and then sip.

Chocolate Protein Smoothie

This smoothie is an excellent option to gain a boost of energy. It also contains a healthy balance of protein, carbohydrates, and healthy fats.

Ingredients:

- 1 banana
- 1/2 cup Greek yogurt
- 1/2 cup of almond milk or milk
- 2 tablespoons of unsweetened cocoa powder
- 2 Tablespoons Protein Powder
- 1 tablespoon honey

Preparation:

- Mix the yogurt, bananas, and milk with protein powder, cocoa powder, honey, and cocoa.
- Blend at the highest speed to blend until it is smooth, approximately 30 minutes.
- If the mixture is thicker, you can add milk and blend it.
- Pour the drink into a glass and then sip.

Blueberry as well as Spinach Smoothie

This smoothie is loaded with antioxidants and vitamins that boost energy. Blueberries are a source of power, and spinach gives you a boost of vitamins.

Ingredients:

- 1 cup frozen blueberries
- 1/2 cup baby spinach
- 1/2 cup Greek yogurt
- 1 cup of coconut water
- 1 tablespoon honey

Preparation:

- Mix the blueberries, spinach coconut water, yogurt, and honey with a mixer.
- Blend at the highest speed to blend until it is smooth. It should take about 30 minutes.
- If the mixture is thicker, you can add coconut water and blend it again.
- Pour it into a glass, and sip.

Strawberry with the Almond Butter Smoothie

This smoothie is an excellent option to gain a boost of energy. It contains a healthy blend of carbohydrates and good fats.

Ingredients:

- 1 Cup frozen strawberry
- 1 banana
- 1/2 cup Greek yogurt
- 1/2 cup of almond milk or milk
- 1 tablespoon almond butter 1 tablespoon almond
- 1 tablespoon honey

Preparation:

- Mix the banana, strawberries yogurt, milk, honey, and almond butter with a blender.
- Blend at high speed until smooth, around 30 minutes.
- If your smoothie seems too thick, pour the milk and blend it again.
- Pour it into a glass, and then sip.

Mango along with Chia Seed Smoothie

This smoothie contains vitamins and minerals that help boost your energy, and chia seeds can increase nutrients and fiber.

Ingredients:

- 1 mango ripe, Peeled, and chopped
- 1/2 cup Greek yogurt
- Half a cup of coconut water
- 1 tablespoon Chia seeds
- 1 tablespoon honey

Preparation:

- Blend in a food processor, and mix the mango, yogurt, coconut water, honey, and chia seeds.
- Blend at a highly high-speed setting until the blend is uniform. It should take about 30 minutes.
- If the mixture is thicker, you can add coconut water and blend it again.
- Pour it into a glass, and then sip.

Green Energy Smoothie

This smoothie is loaded with energy-boosting greens and is an excellent method to take in your daily intake of minerals and vitamins.

Ingredients:

- 1 banana
- 1/2 cup frozen pineapple
- 1/2 cup baby spinach
- 1/2 cup Greek yogurt
- Half a cup of coconut water
- 1 tablespoon honey
- One tablespoon of fresh mint leaves

Preparation:

- Blend in a food processor, mix the pineapple, banana, and spinach with coconut water, yogurt, mint leaves, honey, and.
- Blend at a highly high-speed setting until the blend is uniform. It should take about 30 minutes.
- If the mixture is thicker, you can add coconut water and blend it again.
- Pour the drink into a glass and sip.

Cacao as well as Maca Smoothie

The smoothie is loaded with energy-boosting ingredients, such as the cacao's caffeine maca powder, that can boost endurance and energy levels.

Ingredients:

- 1 banana
- 1/2 cup Greek yogurt
- 1/2 cup of almond milk or milk
- 2 tablespoons cacao powder unsweetened
- 1 cup maca powder
- 1 tablespoon honey

Preparation:

- Blend in a blender. Blend the yogurt, banana, and milk with maca powder, cacao powder, honey, and cacao powder.
- Blend at a high-speed setting until the blend is uniform, approximately 30 minutes.
- If your smoothie seems too thick, pour the milk and blend it again.
- Pour the drink into a glass and sip.

Beets and Berries Smoothie

This smoothie is loaded with ingredients that boost energy levels, including the nitrates found in beets, which improve blood flow, and the fruit's antioxidants.

Ingredients:

- 1 cup of cooked beets chopped
- 1/2 cup frozen mixed berries
- 1/2 cup Greek yogurt
- Half a cup of juice from oranges
- 1 tablespoon honey

Preparation:

- Blend in a food processor, mix the beets, mixed berries, orange juice, yogurt, and honey.
- Blend at the highest speed to blend until it is smooth. It should take about 30 minutes.
- If your smoothie seems too thick, mix in orange juice and blend it again.
- Pour the drink into a glass and sip.

Turmeric as well as Ginger Smoothie

This smoothie is loaded with energy-boosting ingredients, such as turmeric's anti-inflammatory properties and the metabolism-boosting characteristics of ginger.

Ingredients:

- 1 banana
- 1/2 cup Greek yogurt
- 1/2 cup almond or milk milk
- 1 teaspoon ground turmeric
- 1 inches piece of ginger
- 1 tablespoon honey

Preparation:

- Blend in a food processor, and blend the yogurt, banana, milk, and ginger. Add turmeric, ginger, and honey.
- Blend at a high-speed setting until the blend is uniform. It should take about 30 minutes.
- If the mixture is thicker, you can add milk and blend it.
- Pour it into a glass, and sip.

Power Boosting Smoothie

This smoothie contains energy-boosting ingredients, including caffeine from coffee and iron in the spinach.

Ingredients:

- 1 banana
- 1/2 cup Greek yogurt
- 1/2 cup almond or milk milk
- 1 shot espresso or 1/2 cup of strong, strong-brewed coffee
- 1/2 cup spinach
- 1 tablespoon honey

Preparation:

- Blend in a blender. Mix the yogurt, banana coffee, milk, spinach, honey, and coffee.
- Blend at a high-speed setting until the blend is uniform, approximately 30 minutes.
- If the mixture is thicker, you can add milk and blend it.
- Pour it into a glass, and sip.

Apple Pie Smoothie

This smoothie is a deliciously nutritious way to begin your day. It'll give you an extra energy boost and tastes like apple pie.

Ingredients:

- One cup of diced apple
- 1/2 cup Greek yogurt
- 1/2 cup of almond milk or milk
- 1 teaspoon of ground cinnamon
- 1 tablespoon honey
- 1/4 teaspoon vanilla extract

Preparation:

- Blender: mix the apples, yogurt, honey, cinnamon, milk as well as vanilla extract.
- Blend at an extremely high-speed setting until the blend is uniform. It should take about 30 minutes.
- If your smoothie seems too thick, pour the milk and blend it again.
- Pour the drink into a glass and sip.

Avocado and Lime smoothie

This smoothie is a tasty and nutritious way to begin your day. It contains the perfect mix of healthy fats and carbohydrates, giving you a long-lasting energy boost.

Ingredients:

- 1 ripe avocado
- 1/2 cup Greek yogurt
- 1/2 cup almond or milk milk
- One-quarter cup of lime juice
- 1 tablespoon honey
- 1/4 teaspoon vanilla extract

Preparation:

- Blend the avocado milk, yogurt, lime juice, honey, and vanilla extract with a mixer.
- Blend at an extremely high-speed setting until the blend is uniform. It should take about 30 minutes.
- If the mixture is thicker, you can add milk and blend it.
- Pour the drink into a glass and then sip.

Chocolate with a Coconut smoothie

This smoothie is a deliciously nutritious way to begin your day. It contains the perfect combination of healthy fats and carbohydrates that will give you a long-lasting energy boost.

Ingredients:

- 1 banana
- 1/2 cup Greek yogurt
- 1/2 cup coconut milk
- 2 tablespoons of cocoa powder unsweetened
- 1 tablespoon honey
- 1/4 teaspoon of coconut extract

Preparation:

- Blend in a blender. Mix the yogurt, banana cocoa powder, coconut milk, and honey. Add coconut extract.
- Blend at an extremely high-speed setting until the blend is uniform, approximately 30 minutes.
- If your smoothie seems too thick, add more coconut milk and blend it again.
- Pour it into a glass, and then sip.

Cocoa and Peanut Butter Smoothie

This smoothie is a deliciously nutritious way to kick off your day. It has the perfect mix of healthy fats and carbohydrates that will give you energy for the long haul.

Ingredients:

- 1 banana
- 1/2 cup Greek yogurt
- 1/2 cup almond or milk milk
- 2 tablespoons of unsweetened cocoa powder
- Two tablespoons of peanut butter
- 1 tablespoon honey

Preparation:

- Mix the yogurt, banana, cocoa powder, honey, and peanut butter with a blender.
- Blend at the highest speed to blend until it is smooth, approximately 30 minutes.
- If the mixture is thicker, you can add milk and blend it.
- Pour it into a glass, and then sip.

Coconut as well as Banana Smoothie

This smoothie is a tasty, nutritious way to kick off your day. It has an excellent mix of healthy fats and carbohydrates that keep you going for a long time.

Ingredients:

- 1 banana
- 1/2 cup Greek yogurt
- 1/2 cup coconut milk
- 1/4 shredded cup coconut
- 1 tablespoon honey
- 1/4 teaspoon vanilla extract

Preparation:

- With a mixer, mix the ingredients
- Blend at an extremely high-speed setting until the blend is uniform. It should take about 30 minutes.
- If the mixture is thicker, you can add milk and blend it.
- Pour the drink into a glass and sip.

MEAL-REPLENISHMENT SMOOTHIE
Chocolate Peanut Butter Protein Smoothie

This smoothie is a fantastic alternative to an unhealthy meal. It is loaded with healthy fats and protein. It tastes just like the taste of a milkshake with chocolate peanut butter.

Ingredients:

- 1 banana
- 1/2 cup Greek yogurt
- 1/2 cup almond or milk milk
- 2 tablespoons of unsweetened cocoa powder
- 2.25 tablespoons peanut butter
- Two tablespoons of protein powder
- 1 tablespoon honey

Preparation:

- Blender: mix the yogurt, banana, cocoa powder, milk, protein powder, peanut butter, and honey.
- Blend at an extremely high-speed setting until the blend is uniform, approximately 30 minutes.
- If the mixture is thicker, you can add milk and blend it.
- Pour it into a glass, and then sip.

Green Protein Smoothie

This smoothie is loaded with healthy fats, protein, and green leafy vegetables, making it a fantastic alternative to a meal.

Ingredients:

- 1 banana
- 1/2 cup Greek yogurt
- Half a cup of coconut water
- 1/2 cup baby spinach
- 1 tablespoon Chia seeds
- 1 tablespoon hemp seeds
- 2 Tablespoons Protein Powder
- 1 tablespoon honey

Preparation:

- With a blender, blend the yogurt, banana, and coconut water. Add spinach, chia seeds, hemp seeds, protein powder, and honey.
- Blend at the highest speed to blend until it is smooth. It should take about 30 minutes.
- If your smoothie seems too thick, mix in coconut water and blend it again.
- Pour it into a glass, and sip.

Fruit Protein Smoothie

This smoothie contains nutrients, protein, healthy fats, and antioxidants, making it an excellent meal alternative.

Ingredients:

- 1 cup frozen mixed berries
- 1/2 cup Greek yogurt
- 1/2 cup of almond milk or milk
- Two tablespoons of protein powder
- 1 tablespoon Chia seeds
- 1 tablespoon honey

Preparation:

- Blender: blend the berries mixed with yogurt, milk protein powder, chia seeds, and honey.
- Blend at an extremely high-speed setting until the blend is uniform, approximately 30 minutes.
- If the mixture is thicker, you can add milk and blend it again.
- Pour it into a glass, and sip.

A Banana and Oat Smoothie

This smoothie is an excellent option to substitute an unhealthy meal. It is full of nutrients and fiber and keeps you full for several hours.

Ingredients:

- 1 banana
- 1/2 cup of rolled Oats
- 1/2 cup Greek yogurt
- 1/2 cup of almond milk or milk
- 2 Tablespoons Protein Powder
- 1 tablespoon honey
- 1/4 teaspoon vanilla extract

Preparation:

- Mix the banana, oatmeal milk, yogurt honey, protein powder, and vanilla extract with a mixer.
- Blend at an extremely high-speed setting until the blend is uniform. It should take about 30 minutes.
- If the mixture is thicker, you can add milk and blend it again.
- Pour it into a glass, and sip.

The Chocolate-covered Strawberry Smoothie

This smoothie is a delicious and healthy alternative to eating a healthy meal loaded with protein and antioxidants.

Ingredients:

- 1 Cup frozen strawberry
- 1 banana
- 1/2 cup Greek yogurt
- 1/2 cup almond or milk milk
- 2 tablespoons of unsweetened cocoa powder
- 2 Tablespoons Protein Powder
- 1 tablespoon honey

Preparation:

- Blender: mix the banana, strawberries, milk, yogurt, and cocoa powder. Add protein powder, honey, and.
- Blend at an extremely high-speed setting until the blend is uniform. It should take about 30 minutes.
- If the mixture is thicker, you can add milk and blend it again.
- Pour the drink into a glass and sip.

Superfood Smoothie

This smoothie is loaded with superfoods and will leave you full and happy for long hours.

Ingredients:

- 1 banana
- 1/2 cup Greek yogurt
- Half a cup of coconut water
- 1/4 cup frozen blueberries
- 1 tablespoon Chia seeds
- 1 tablespoon goji berries
- Two tablespoons of protein powder
- 1 tablespoon honey

Preparation:

- With a blender, mix the yogurt, banana, and coconut water. Add blueberries, Chia seeds, Goji berries and honey, protein powder, and.
- Blend at an extremely high-speed setting until the blend is uniform. It should take about 30 minutes.
- If the mixture is thicker, you can add coconut water and blend it again.
- Pour the drink into a glass and then sip.

Avocado and Mango Smoothie

This smoothie is a tasty and healthy alternative to a meal packed with nutritious fats and antioxidants.

Ingredients:

- 1 ripe avocado
- 1 mango ripe Peeled, and chopped
- 1/2 cup Greek yogurt
- 1 cup of coconut water
- 1 tablespoon Chia seeds
- 1 tablespoon honey

Preparation:

- Blend in a food processor, blend the mango, avocado yogurt, coconut water, yogurt, honey, chia seeds, and
- Blend at an extremely high-speed setting until the blend is uniform. It should take about 30 minutes.
- If the mixture is thicker, you can add coconut water and blend again.
- Pour it into a glass, and sip.

Chocolate Banana Protein Smoothie

This smoothie is a tasty and healthy meal replacement loaded with healthy fats, protein, and antioxidants.

Ingredients:

- 1 banana
- 1/2 cup Greek yogurt
- 1/2 cup of almond milk or milk
- 2 tablespoons of unsweetened cocoa powder
- 2 Tablespoons Protein Powder
- 1 tablespoon honey

Preparation:

- Blender: blend the yogurt, banana, and milk with protein powder, cocoa powder, honey, and cocoa.
- Blend at an extremely high-speed setting until the blend is uniform. It should take about 30 minutes.
- If your smoothie seems too thick, pour the milk and blend it again.
- Pour it into a glass, and then sip.

Spinach with Banana Protein Smoothie

This smoothie is a delicious and healthy meal replacement loaded with proteins, healthy fats, and antioxidants.

Ingredients:

- 1 banana
- 1/2 cup Greek yogurt
- 1/2 cup of almond milk or milk
- 1/2 cup baby spinach
- 2 Tablespoons Protein Powder
- 1 tablespoon honey

Preparation:

- Blend the yogurt, banana, spinach, milk protein powder, and honey with a mixer.
- Blend at an extremely high-speed setting until the blend is uniform, approximately 30 minutes.
- If your smoothie seems too thick, pour the milk and blend it again.
- Pour the drink into a glass and sip.

Carrot as well as orange Protein Smoothie

This smoothie is a delicious meal replacement loaded with healthy fats, protein, and antioxidants.

Ingredients:

- 1 cup chopped carrots
- 1/2 cup Greek yogurt
- 1 cup of orange juice
- 2 Tablespoons Protein Powder
- 1 tablespoon honey
- 1/4 teaspoon vanilla extract

Preparation:

- Blender: mix with yogurt, carrots, protein powder, orange juice, honey, and vanilla extract.
- Blend at an extremely high-speed setting until the blend is uniform, approximately 30 minutes.
- If the drink is thick enough, you can add orange juice and blend it again.
- Pour the drink into a glass and sip.

Peanut Butter and Banana Smoothie

This smoothie is a delicious and healthy alternative to eating a healthy meal loaded with nutrients, protein, and healthy fats.

Ingredients:

- 1 banana
- 1/2 cup Greek yogurt
- 1/2 cup almond or milk milk
- 2.25 tablespoons peanut butter
- 2 Tablespoons Protein Powder
- 1 tablespoon honey
- 1/4 teaspoon vanilla extract

Preparation:

- With a mixer, blend the yogurt, banana, peanut butter, milk, honey, protein powder, and vanilla extract.
- Blend at the highest speed to blend until it is smooth, approximately 30 minutes.
- If the mixture is thicker, you can add milk and blend it again.
- Pour it into a glass, and then sip.

Strawberry as well as Oat Smoothie

This smoothie is a tasty and healthy alternative to a meal loaded with antioxidants and fiber.

Ingredients:

- 1 Cup frozen strawberry
- 1/2 cup Greek yogurt
- 1/2 cup of almond milk or milk
- 2 tablespoons of rolled oats
- Two tablespoons of protein powder
- 1 tablespoon honey

Preparation:

- Mix the yogurt, strawberries, and milk, Oats, protein powder, and honey with a blender.
- Blend at the highest speed to blend until it is smooth, approximately 30 minutes.
- If the mixture is thicker, you can add milk and blend it.
- Pour the drink into a glass and sip.

Blueberry with Greek Yogurt Smoothie

This smoothie is a delicious and healthy alternative to a meal loaded with antioxidants and protein.

Ingredients:

- 1 cup frozen blueberries
- 1/2 cup Greek yogurt
- 1/2 cup of almond milk or milk
- 2 tablespoons honey
- 1/4 teaspoon vanilla extract

Preparation:

- Blend in a food processor, and blend your blueberries with yogurt, honey, milk, and vanilla extract.
- Blend at the highest speed to blend until it is smooth, approximately 30 minutes.
- If the mixture is thicker, you can add milk and blend it.
- Pour it into a glass, and sip.

Chocolate, as well as the Almond Butter Smoothie

This smoothie is a delicious and healthy meal replacement loaded with proteins, healthy fats, and antioxidants.

Ingredients:

- 1 banana
- 1/2 cup Greek yogurt
- 1/2 cup almond or milk milk
- 2 tablespoons of unsweetened cocoa powder
- Two tablespoons of almond butter
- 2 Tablespoons Protein Powder
- 1 tablespoon honey

Preparation:

- Blender: mix the yogurt, banana, cocoa powder, almond butter, protein powder, and honey.
- Blend at the highest speed to blend until it is smooth, approximately 30 minutes.
- If your smoothie seems too thick, pour the milk and blend it again.
- Pour it into a glass, and then sip.

Pineapple as well as Coconut Smoothie

This smoothie is a delicious and healthy meal replacement packed with antioxidants and healthy fats.

Ingredients:

- 1 cup of frozen or fresh pineapple
- 1/2 cup Greek yogurt
- 1/2 cup coconut milk
- 2 tablespoons of coconut that has been shredded
- Two tablespoons of protein powder
- 1 tablespoon honey

Preparation:

- Mix the yogurt, pineapple coconut milk, coconut shredded protein powder, and honey in a food processor.
- Blend at an extremely high-speed setting until the blend is uniform, approximately 30 minutes.
- If the drink is thick enough, you can add more coconut milk and blend again.
- Pour the drink into a glass and then sip.

DETOXIFYING AND CLEANSING SMOOTHIE
Green Detox Smoothie

This smoothie is loaded with nutritious greens and fruits, which help detoxify and cleanse the body.

Ingredients:

- 1/2 cup kale or spinach
- 1/2 cup of cucumber
- 1/2 cup pineapple
- 1/2 cup green apples
- 1/2 avocado
- 1/4 cup mint leaves
- 1-inch ginger
- 1/2 cup of coconut or water water

Preparation:

- Mix the spinach or kale, pineapple, cucumber, avocado, green apples, ginger, mint leaves, and coconut water with a blender.
- Blend at an extremely high-speed setting until the blend is uniform, approximately 30 minutes.
- If your smoothie seems too thick, pour in water and blend it again.
- Pour the drink into a glass and then sip.

Lemon and Ginger Smoothie

This smoothie is loaded with ginger and lemon, renowned for its cleansing and detoxifying properties.

Ingredients:

- 1 lemon juiced
- 1-inch ginger
- 1/2 cup Greek yogurt
- Half a cup of coconut water
- 1/2 cup frozen berries
- 1 tablespoon honey

Preparation:

- With a blender, mix the juice of lemon and ginger and yogurt with coconut water, coconut frozen berries, and honey.
- Blend at the highest speed to blend until it is smooth. It should take about 30 minutes.
- If the mixture is thicker, you can add coconut water and blend it again.
- Pour it into a glass, and sip.

Beet as well as Berry Cleansing Smoothie

This smoothie is loaded with berries and beets that are well-known for their cleansing and detoxifying properties.

Ingredients:

- Half-cup beets cooked
- 1/2 cup frozen berries
- 1/2 cup Greek yogurt
- Half a cup of coconut water
- 1 tablespoon honey
- 1/4 teaspoon vanilla extract

Preparation:

- Blend in a food processor, mix the cooked beets, frozen berries, coconut water, yogurt, vanilla extract, honey and.
- Blend at an extremely high-speed setting until the blend is uniform, approximately 30 minutes.
- If the mixture is thicker, you can add coconut water and blend it again.
- Pour the drink into a glass and then sip.

Apple Detox and Cabbage Smoothie

This smoothie is loaded with apples and cabbage, known for its cleansing and detoxifying properties.

Ingredients:

- 1/2 cup chopped cabbage
- 1/2 cup green apples
- 1/2 cup Greek yogurt
- Half a cup of coconut water
- 1 tablespoon honey
- 1/4 teaspoon of cinnamon

Preparation:

- With a mixer, blend the ingredients
- Blend at an extremely high-speed setting until the blend is uniform, approximately 30 minutes.
- If the mixture is thicker, you can add coconut water and blend it again.
- Pour the drink into a glass and then sip.

Ginger as well as Turmeric Smoothie

This smoothie is stuffed with turmeric and ginger, both of which have detoxifying and anti-inflammatory properties.

Ingredients:

- 1-inch ginger
- 1 teaspoon turmeric powder
- 1/2 cup Greek yogurt
- Half a cup of coconut water
- 1/2 cup frozen pineapple
- 1 tablespoon honey
- 1/4 teaspoon vanilla extract

Preparation:

- With a mixer, blend the turmeric powder, ginger, and yogurt with coconut water, coconut, frozen pineapples, honey, and vanilla extract.
- Blend at an extremely high-speed setting until the blend is uniform, approximately 30 minutes.
- If your smoothie seems too thick, mix in coconut water and blend again.
- Pour it into a glass, and then sip.

Cilantro with Lemon Detox Smoothie

This smoothie is loaded with lime and cilantro, renowned for their cleansing properties.

Ingredients:

- 1/4 cup cilantro leaves
- 1 lime that has been juiced
- 1/2 cup Greek yogurt
- 1 cup of coconut water
- 1/2 cup frozen berries
- 1 tablespoon honey
- 1/4 teaspoon vanilla extract

Preparation:

- Mix the lime juice, cilantro, coconut water, yogurt, and frozen berries with a blender. Add vanilla extract, honey and.
- Blend at the highest speed to blend until it is smooth, approximately 30 minutes.
- If the mixture is thicker, you can add coconut water and blend it again.
- Pour the drink into a glass and sip.

Culver and celery Smoothie to Detox

This smoothie is loaded with celery and cucumber, renowned for their cleansing properties.

Ingredients:

- 1/2 cup of cucumber
- 1/2 cup of celery
- 1/2 cup Greek yogurt
- Half a cup of coconut water
- 1/2 cup frozen pineapple
- 1 tablespoon honey
- 1/4 teaspoon vanilla extract

Preparation:

- Blend the celery, cucumber, coconut water, yogurt honey, frozen pineapple, and vanilla extract with a blender.
- Blend at an extremely high-speed setting until the blend is uniform. It should take about 30 minutes.
- If the mixture is thicker, you can add coconut water and blend again.
- Pour the drink into a glass and sip.

Beet as well as Carrot Detox Smoothie

This smoothie is loaded with carrots and beets, both of which have detoxifying properties.

Ingredients:

- 1 cup of cooked beets
- 1/2 cup of carrots
- 1/2 cup Greek yogurt
- Half a cup of coconut water
- 1/2 cup frozen berries
- 1 tablespoon honey
- 1/4 teaspoon vanilla extract

Preparation:

- Blend in a food processor, and blend the carrots, beets, coconut water, yogurt, frozen fruit, honey, and vanilla extract.
- Blend at an extremely high-speed setting until the blend is uniform, approximately 30 minutes.
- If your smoothie seems too thick, mix in coconut water and blend again.
- Pour the drink into a glass and sip.

Spinach along with Kale Detox Smoothie

This smoothie is loaded with kale and spinach, which have cleansing properties.

Ingredients:

- 1/2 cup spinach leaves
- 1/2 cup of kale leaves
- 1/2 cup Greek yogurt
- 1 cup of coconut water
- 1/2 cup frozen pineapple
- 1 tablespoon honey
- 1/4 teaspoon vanilla extract

Preparation:

- Blend in a food processor, blend the kale, spinach, coconut water, yogurt, frozen pineapples, honey, and vanilla extract.
- Blend at an extremely high-speed setting until the blend is uniform, approximately 30 minutes.
- If your smoothie seems too thick, mix in coconut water and blend again.
- Pour the drink into a glass and sip.

Lemon and ginger Smoothie for Detox

This smoothie is loaded with ginger and lemon, both of which have detoxifying properties.

Ingredients:

- 1/2 lemon juiced
- 1-inch ginger
- 1/2 cup Greek yogurt
- 1 cup of coconut water
- 1/2 cup frozen berries
- 1 tablespoon honey
- 1/4 teaspoon vanilla extract

Preparation:

- Blend in a food processor, and mix the juice of lemon, ginger, and yogurt. Add coconut water, coconut milk, frozen berries, vanilla extract, honey and.
- Blend at the highest speed to blend until it is smooth, approximately 30 minutes.
- If the mixture is thicker, you can add coconut water and blend it again.
- Pour it into a glass, and sip.

Cucumber and Mint Detox Smoothie

This smoothie is loaded with mint and cucumber, which have detoxifying properties.

Ingredients:

- 1/2 cup cucumber peeled and diced
- 1/4 cup fresh mint leaves
- 1/2 cup Greek yogurt
- Half a cup of coconut water
- 1/2 cup frozen berries
- 1 tablespoon honey
- 1/4 teaspoon vanilla extract

Preparation:

- Blend in a food processor and blend the mint, cucumber, yogurt, coconut water, and frozen berries. Add vanilla extract, honey and.
- Blend at an extremely high-speed setting until the blend is uniform, approximately 30 minutes.
- If your smoothie seems too thick, mix in coconut water and blend it again.
- Pour the drink into a glass and sip.

Chia as well as Flaxseed Detox Smoothie

This smoothie is loaded with flaxseed and chia, known for their cleansing properties.

Ingredients:

- 1 tablespoon Chia seeds
- 1 tablespoon flaxseed
- 1/2 cup Greek yogurt
- Half a cup of coconut water
- 1/2 cup frozen berries
- 1 tablespoon honey
- 1/4 teaspoon vanilla extract

Preparation:

- Blend in a food processor and mix the flaxseed, chia seeds, coconut water, yogurt, frozen berries, vanilla extract, and honey.
- Blend at the highest speed to blend until it is smooth. It should take about 30 minutes.
- If the mixture is thicker, you can add coconut water and blend again.
- Pour it into a glass, and then sip.

Avocado as well as Banana Smoothie to detox

This smoothie is loaded with avocado and bananas, renowned for their detoxifying qualities.

Ingredients:

- 1/2 avocado
- 1 banana
- 1/2 cup Greek yogurt
- 1 cup of coconut water
- 1/2 cup frozen berries
- 1 tablespoon honey
- 1/4 teaspoon vanilla extract

Preparation:

- Blend in a food processor, and blend ingredients such as avocado, banana, coconut water, yogurt, and frozen berries. Add vanilla extract, honey and.
- Blend at an extremely high-speed setting until the blend is uniform. It should take about 30 minutes.
- If the mixture is thicker, you can add coconut water and blend again.
- Pour the drink into a glass and then sip.

Turmeric and ginger Detox Smoothie

This smoothie is loaded with ginger and turmeric, which are well-known for their detoxifying properties.

Ingredients:

- 1 tablespoon turmeric powder
- 1-inch ginger grated
- 1/2 cup Greek yogurt
- Half a cup of coconut water
- 1/2 cup frozen berries
- 1 tablespoon honey
- 1/4 teaspoon vanilla extract

Preparation:

- Blend in a food processor, and mix the turmeric powder with ginger, coconut water, yogurt, frozen berries, vanilla extract, and honey.
- Blend at the highest speed to blend until it is smooth, approximately 30 minutes.
- If the mixture is thicker, you can add coconut water and blend it again.
- Pour it into a glass, and then sip.

Lemon and Ginger Smoothie

This smoothie is filled with ginger and lemon, renowned for their cleansing properties.

Ingredients:

- Juice from 1 lemon
- 1-inch ginger grated
- 1/2 cup Greek yogurt
- Half a cup of coconut water
- 1/2 cup frozen berries
- 1 tablespoon honey
- 1/4 teaspoon vanilla extract

Preparation:

- With a blender, mix the juice of a lemon with ginger yogurt, coconut water, yogurt, and frozen berries. Add vanilla extract and honey.
- Blend at the highest speed to blend until it is smooth. It should take about 30 minutes.
- If the mixture is thicker, you can add coconut water and blend again.
- Pour the drink into a glass and then sip.

Vegan Smoothie Detox

1. Add Green
2. Add Fruits
3. Add Liquid
4. Booster

VEGETABLE AND VEGAN SMOOTHIES

Green Goddess Smoothie

This smoothie is stuffed with greens, which makes it a fantastic method to take in your daily intake of veggies.

Ingredients:

- 1 cup spinach
- 1/2 cup of kale
- 1/2 avocado
- 1/2 cup coconut milk
- 1/2 cup frozen pineapple
- 1/2 lime and juiced
- 1/4 teaspoon vanilla extract

Preparation:

- With a blender, blend the kale, spinach coconut milk, avocado chilled pineapples, lime juice, and vanilla extract.
- Blend at an extremely high-speed setting until the blend is uniform. It should take about 30 minutes.
- If the drink is thick enough, you can add more coconut milk and blend again.
- Pour it into a glass, and then sip.

Carrot as well as Ginger Smoothie

This smoothie is loaded with ginger and carrots, which have anti-inflammatory properties.

Ingredients:

- 1 cup carrots peeled and diced
- 1/2 inch ginger grated
- 1/2 cup coconut milk
- 1/2 cup frozen mango
- 1/4 teaspoon vanilla extract

Preparation:

- With a blender, blend the carrots, ginger mango, coconut milk, frozen mango, and vanilla extract.
- Blend at the highest speed to blend until it is smooth, approximately 30 minutes.
- If the drink is thick enough, add coconut milk and blend again.
- Pour the drink into a glass and then sip.

Sweet Potato Smoothie

This smoothie is made from sweet potatoes, a fantastic food source for complex carbs. They also add a natural sweetness to the drink.

Ingredients:

- 1 cup cooked sweet potato
- 1 cup coconut milk
- 1/2 cup frozen berries
- 1 tablespoon maple syrup 1 tablespoon maple syrup
- 1/4 teaspoon vanilla extract

Preparation:

- Blend in a food processor, and mix the sweet potato coconut milk, frozen berries, vanilla syrup, and maple syrup. Extract.
- Blend at an extremely high-speed setting until the blend is uniform, approximately 30 minutes.
- If the drink is thick enough, you can add more coconut milk and blend it again.
- Pour it into a glass, and sip.

Cucumber as well as Mint Smoothie

This smoothie is made of mint and cucumber. Both are famous for their refreshing and hydrating properties.

Ingredients:

- 1 cup cucumber peeled and diced
- 1/4 cup mint leaves
- 1/2 cup coconut milk
- 1/2 cup frozen pineapple
- 1/4 teaspoon vanilla extract

Preparation:

- With a blender, blend the mint, cucumber Coconut milk, pineapple frozen, and vanilla extract.
- Blend at an extremely high-speed setting until the blend is uniform. It should take about 30 minutes.
- If the drink is thick enough, add coconut milk and blend again.
- Pour it into a glass, and then sip.

Broccoli along with Apple Smoothie

This smoothie is loaded with broccoli, rich in vitamin C and fiber, and apples, a fantastic food source for antioxidants.

Ingredients:

- 1 cup broccoli with florets
- 1 apple Cored and diced
- 1/2 cup coconut milk
- 1/2 cup frozen berries
- 1/4 teaspoon vanilla extract

Preparation:

- Blend in a food processor and mix the apple, broccoli coconut milk, frozen blueberries, and vanilla extract.
- Blend at the highest speed to blend until it is smooth. It should take about 30 minutes.
- If your smoothie seems too thick, add more coconut milk and blend it again.
- Pour the drink into a glass and sip.

Beet as well as Berry Smoothie

It is made from beets, which are rich in iron, antioxidants, and berries, an excellent food source for vitamin C.

Ingredients:

- Half-cup beets cooked
- 1/2 cup frozen berries
- 1/2 cup coconut milk
- Half a cup of juice from oranges
- 1/4 teaspoon vanilla extract

Preparation:

- With a blender, mix the beets, frozen berries, Coconut milk, juice of an orange along with vanilla extract.
- Blend at the highest speed to blend until it is smooth, approximately 30 minutes.
- If your smoothie seems too thick, you can add more coconut milk and then blend again.
- Pour the drink into a glass and then sip.

Kale along with Apple Smoothie

This smoothie is loaded with kale high in vitamins K A, C, and K, and apples, a fantastic food source for antioxidants.

Ingredients:

- 1 cup of kale
- 1 apple Cored and diced
- 1/2 cup coconut milk
- 1/2 cup frozen pineapple
- 1/4 teaspoon vanilla extract

Preparation:

- Blend in a food processor, blend the kale, apple, coconut milk, frozen pineapple, and vanilla extract.
- Blend at an extremely high-speed setting until the blend is uniform, approximately 30 minutes.
- If your smoothie seems too thick, add coconut milk and blend again.
- Pour it into a glass, and then sip.

The Banana Squash Smoothie and the Squash

The smoothie was made of squash which is rich in potassium and vitamin A, as well as bananas, which are an excellent source of potassium and fiber.

Ingredients:

- 1 cup of cooked butternut squash
- 1 banana
- 1/2 cup coconut milk
- 1/2 cup frozen berries
- 1/4 teaspoon vanilla extract

Preparation:

- With a food processor, mix the butternut squash, bananas, frozen coconut milk, and vanilla extract.
- Blend at the highest speed to blend until it is smooth. It should take about 30 minutes.
- If the drink is thick enough, you can add more coconut milk and blend it again.
- Pour it into a glass, and sip.

Spinach and Cucumber Smoothie

This smoothie is loaded with spinach which is rich in iron, vitamins K, A, and cucumber, which is abundant in antioxidants and hydration.

Ingredients:

- 1 cup spinach leaves
- 1/2 cucumber peeled and chopped
- 1/2 cup coconut milk
- 1/2 cup frozen pineapple
- 1/4 teaspoon vanilla extract

Preparation:

- With a blender, blend the spinach leaves, cucumber, coconut milk, frozen pineapple, and vanilla extract.
- Blend at an extremely high-speed setting until the blend is uniform. It should take about 30 minutes.
- If the drink is thick enough, add coconut milk and blend again.
- Pour it into a glass, and then sip.

Carrot as well as Ginger Smoothie

This smoothie is made from carrots which are abundant in vitamin A. Also, there is ginger. It is famous for its anti-inflammatory qualities.

Ingredients:

- 1 Cup cooked and cooked carrots
- 1-inch piece of ginger removed and grated
- 1/2 cup coconut milk
- 1/2 cup frozen berries
- 1/4 teaspoon vanilla extract

Preparation:

- With a food processor, blend ginger, carrots, coconut milk, frozen fruits, and vanilla extract.
- Blend at the highest speed to blend until it is smooth, approximately 30 minutes.
- If your smoothie seems too thick, add coconut milk and blend again.

Pour it into a glass, and sip.

Cauliflower along with Banana Smoothie

The smoothie was made from the cauliflower plant, rich in vitamins C and K, as well as bananas, which are excellent sources of potassium.

Ingredients:

- 1 cup cauliflower with florets
- 1 banana
- 1/2 cup coconut milk
- 1/2 cup frozen berries
- 1/4 teaspoon vanilla extract

Preparation:

- With a blender, blend the cauliflower florets with banana coconut milk, frozen berries, and vanilla extract.
- Blend at the highest speed to blend until it is smooth, approximately 30 minutes.
- If the drink is thick enough, add coconut milk and blend again.
- Pour it into a glass, and sip.

Kale along with Pineapple Smoothie

This smoothie is made from Kale, which is abundant in calcium and iron, and pineapple, which is abundant in vitamins C and bromelain. It is an enzyme that assists digestion.

Ingredients:

- 1 cup of kale leaves
- 1/2 cup pineapple chunks
- 1/2 cup coconut milk
- 1/2 cup frozen berries
- 1/4 teaspoon vanilla extract

Preparation:

- With a blender, mix the leaves of kale, pineapple chunks, frozen berries, and coconut milk along with vanilla extract.
- Blend at an extremely high-speed setting until the blend is uniform, approximately 30 minutes.
- If the drink is thick enough, you can add more coconut milk and blend again.
- Pour it into a glass, and then sip.

Broccoli along with Apple Smoothie

The smoothie is made using broccoli abundant in vitamins K and C, and apples, which are packed with antioxidants and fiber.

Ingredients:

- 1 cup of broccoli.
- 1 apple Cored and diced
- 1/2 cup coconut milk
- 1/2 cup frozen berries
- 1/4 teaspoon vanilla extract

Preparation:

- With a blender, blend the broccoli florets with apple, coconut milk, frozen fruits, and vanilla extract.
- Blend at an extremely high-speed setting until the blend is uniform. It should take about 30 minutes.
- If the drink is thick enough, you can add more coconut milk and blend it again.
- Pour the drink into a glass and sip.

Mango and Squash Smoothies

The smoothie is made using squash, which is abundant in Vitamin A, fiber, and mango. Mango is abundant in Vitamin C and antioxidants.

Ingredients:

- 1 cup cooked squash
- 1 mango peeled and diced
- 1/2 cup coconut milk
- 1/4 teaspoon vanilla extract

Preparation:

- With a mixer, blend the mango, squash coconut milk, the mango along with vanilla extract.
- Blend at the highest speed to blend until it is smooth, approximately 30 minutes.
- If the drink is thick enough, add coconut milk and blend it again.
- Pour it into a glass, and then sip.

Spinach as well as Avocado Smoothie

This smoothie is made from spinach which happens to be rich in vitamins K, A, and C, as well as avocado which is rich in healthy fiber and fats.

Ingredients:

- 1 cup spinach leaves
- 1 avocado peeled and diced
- 1/2 cup coconut milk
- 1/2 cup frozen berries
- 1/4 teaspoon vanilla extract

Preparation:

- Blender: blend the spinach leaves, avocado, coconut milk, frozen berries, coconut milk, and vanilla extract.
- Blend at an extremely high-speed setting until the blend is uniform, approximately 30 minutes.
- If your smoothie seems too thick, add more coconut milk and blend it again.
- Pour the drink into a glass and then sip.

ANTI-AGING SMOOTHIES

Blueberry as well as Acai Smoothie

This drink is loaded with antioxidants from blueberries and acai berries, which fight free radicals and help slow the process of aging.

Ingredients:

- 1/2 cup frozen blueberries
- 1/2 cup frozen acai berries
- 1/2 cup Greek yogurt
- 1 cup almond milk
- 1/4 teaspoon honey

Preparation:

- Mix the frozen blueberries and acai-like berries in a food processor. Add Greek yogurt along with almond milk and honey.
- Blend at the highest speed to blend until it is smooth, approximately 30 minutes.
- If your smoothie seems too thick, add almond milk and blend it again.
- Pour it into a glass, and then sip.

The Pomegranate, Green Tea Smoothie

Pomegranates are rich in antioxidants. Green tea is also high in anti-inflammatory and antioxidants that fight free radicals and slow the process of aging.

Ingredients:

- 1/2 cup pomegranate juice
- 1/2 cup of green tea that has been brewed
- 1/2 cup frozen berries
- 1/4 cup Greek yogurt
- 1/4 teaspoon honey

Preparation:

- Blend in a blender. Blend the juice of pomegranate as well as green tea, frozen fruit, Greek yogurt, and honey.
- Blend at an extremely high-speed setting until the blend is uniform. It should take about 30 minutes.
- If your smoothie seems too thick, you can make it thinner by adding more pomegranate juice. Mix again.
- Pour it into a glass, and then sip.

Strawberry as well as Kale Smoothie

It is made of strawberries, which happen to be rich in vitamin C. It also contains the kale plant, which is rich in antioxidants. These keep your skin looking youthful and healthy.

Ingredients:

- 1 cup of fresh Kale
- 1 Cup of frozen strawberries
- 1/2 cup Greek yogurt
- One cup of almond milk
- 1/4 teaspoon honey

Preparation:

- With a blender, blend fresh kale, frozen strawberries, Greek yogurt, almond milk, and honey.
- Blend at an extremely high-speed setting until the blend is uniform. It should take about 30 minutes.
- If your smoothie seems too thick, add more almond milk and then blend it again.
- Pour it into a glass, and then sip.

Papaya as well as Pineapple Smoothie

Papaya is a source of an enzyme known as papain, which assists in removing dead skin cells. Also, pineapple is rich in vitamin C and bromelain. It is an enzyme that assists in reducing inflammation.

Ingredients:

- 1 cup papaya Peeled and diced
- 1 cup frozen pineapple
- 1/2 cup coconut milk
- 1/4 cup Greek yogurt
- 1/4 teaspoon honey

Preparation:

- Blend in a food processor, mix the frozen pineapple, papaya, coconut milk, Greek yogurt, honey, and.
- Blend at an extremely high-speed setting until the blend is uniform. It should take about 30 minutes.
- If the drink is thick enough, you can add more coconut milk and blend it again.
- Pour it into a glass, and sip.

Avocado as well as Spinach Smoothie

The smoothie is made of avocado, a fantastic source of antioxidants and healthy fats, and the spinach plant, famous for its rich vitamin C and A levels and its anti-aging properties.

Ingredients:

- 1/2 avocado
- 1 cup fresh spinach leaves
- Half a cup of almond milk
- 1/2 cup frozen berries
- 1 tablespoon honey
- 1/4 teaspoon vanilla extract

Preparation:

- With a blender, blend ingredients such as the avocado, the leaves of spinach, almond milk, fresh berries frozen, honey as well as vanilla extract.
- Blend at an extremely high-speed setting until the blend is uniform. It should take about 30 minutes.
- If the drink is thick enough, add almond milk and blend it again.
- Pour the drink into a glass and then sip.

Turmeric as well as Ginger Smoothie

The smoothie is made up of ginger and turmeric. They are each recognized for their anti-inflammatory as well as antioxidant properties. They are perfect for fighting the signs of aging.

Ingredients:

- 1 teaspoon ground turmeric
- 1 teaspoon ginger grated
- 1/2 cup coconut milk
- 1/2 cup frozen pineapple
- 1 tablespoon honey
- 1/4 teaspoon vanilla extract

Preparation:

- Mix the ginger, turmeric coconut milk, fresh pineapple, honey, and vanilla extract with a mixer.
- Blend at an extremely high-speed setting until the blend is uniform, approximately 30 minutes.
- If your smoothie seems too thick, add coconut milk and blend it again.
- Pour it into a glass, and then sip.

Blueberry as well as Kale Smoothie

This smoothie is made from blueberries, known for their antioxidants and anti-inflammatory properties. Also, there is Kale, which is famous due to its vitamin K, vitamin C content, and anti-aging properties.

Ingredients:

- 1/2 cup blueberries
- 1 cup of kale leaves
- Half a cup of almond milk
- Half cup peaches frozen
- 1 tablespoon honey
- 1/4 teaspoon vanilla extract

Preparation:

- Blend in a food processor, mix the blueberries, kale leaves, almond milk, peaches frozen vanilla extract, honey and.
- Blend at the highest speed to blend until it is smooth. It should take about 30 minutes.
- If your smoothie seems too thick, add almond milk and blend again.
- Pour it into a glass, and sip.

Pomegranate and Flaxseed Smoothie

This smoothie is made from the pomegranate plant, recognized for its high antioxidant and anti-inflammatory properties, and flaxseed, which is famous for its high omega-3 and anti-aging properties.

Ingredients:

- 1/2 cup of pomegranate seeds
- 1 cup ground flaxseed
- 1/2 cup coconut milk
- 1/2 cup frozen pineapple
- 1 tablespoon honey
- 1/4 teaspoon vanilla extract

Preparation:

- Mix the seeds of pomegranate flaxseed, coconut milk, flaxseed, frozen pineapples, honey, and vanilla extract.
- Blend at an extremely high-speed setting until the blend is uniform, approximately 30 minutes.
- In case the drink is thick enough, you can add more coconut milk and then blend it again.
- Pour it into a glass, and then sip.

Goji Berries along with Almond Smoothie

This smoothie is made from Goji berries, recognized for their high antioxidants and their anti-inflammatory qualities, and almonds. It is popular because of its rich vitamin E content and anti-aging properties.

Ingredients:

- 1/4 cup goji berries
- 1/4 cup almonds
- Half a cup of almond milk
- 1/2 cup frozen mango
- 1 tablespoon honey
- 1/4 teaspoon vanilla extract

Preparation:

- Blend in a food processor, blend the Goji berries, almonds, mango, almond milk, honey, and vanilla extract.
- Blend at an extremely high-speed setting until the blend is uniform, approximately 30 minutes.
- If the drink is thick enough, you can add more almond milk and blend it again.
- Pour it into a glass, and sip.

Acai along with Strawberry Smoothie

This drink is made from Acai berries, which are well-known for their antioxidants and anti-inflammatory qualities, and strawberries, popular for their high vitamin C content and anti-aging properties.

Ingredients:

- 1/4 cup acai berries
- 1/2 cup fresh strawberries
- 1 cup almond milk
- 1/2 cup frozen bananas
- 1 tablespoon honey
- 1/4 teaspoon vanilla extract

Preparation:

- With a blender, mix the Acai berries, strawberries, frozen bananas, almond milk, honey, and vanilla extract.
- Blend at the highest speed to blend until it is smooth. It should take about 30 minutes.
- If the drink is thick enough, add almond milk and blend it again.
- Pour it into a glass, and then sip.

Chia, along with Raspberry Smoothie

This drink is made of Chia seeds, well-known for their omega-3 content and anti-aging properties. Then there are raspberries, known for their antioxidant content and anti-inflammatory properties.

Ingredients:

- 1 tablespoon Chia seeds
- 1 cup of fresh raspberry berries
- 1/2 cup coconut milk
- 1 cup of frozen strawberry slices
- 1 tablespoon honey
- 1/4 teaspoon vanilla extract

Preparation:

- With a blender, mix the raspberries, chia seeds, frozen strawberries, and coconut milk with honey as well as vanilla extract.
- Blend at an extremely high-speed setting until the blend is uniform, approximately 30 minutes.
- If the drink is thick enough, add coconut milk and blend it again.
- Pour the drink into a glass and then sip.

Turmeric as well as Pineapple Smoothie

The smoothie is made from the spice turmeric, which is famous due to its properties in reducing inflammation as well as its capacity to shield against age-related illnesses the fruit of the pineapple is famous for its high levels of vitamin C and its ability to boost collagen production.

Ingredients:

- 1 teaspoon turmeric powder
- 1/2 cup fresh pineapple
- 1/2 cup coconut milk
- 1/2 cup frozen mango
- 1 tablespoon honey
- 1/4 teaspoon vanilla extract

Preparation:

- Blend in a blender. Mix the pineapple, turmeric powder, coconut milk, frozen mango, and honey along with vanilla extract.
- Blend at the highest speed to blend until it is smooth. It should take about 30 minutes.
- If your smoothie seems too thick, add coconut milk and blend again.
- Pour the drink into a glass and sip.

Beet with Blueberry Smoothie

This smoothie is made from beets, which are famous for their antioxidant content and capacity to boost blood flow, and blueberries, well-known for their antioxidant content and ability to fight off age-related illnesses.

Ingredients:

- 1/2 cup beetroot
- 1/2 cup fresh blueberries
- Half a cup of almond milk
- 1 cup of frozen strawberry slices
- 1 tablespoon honey
- 1/4 teaspoon vanilla extract

Preparation:

- Blender: mix the blueberries, beetroots, and almond milk. Add fresh strawberries and honey as well as vanilla extract.
- Blend at an extremely high-speed setting until the blend is uniform, approximately 30 minutes.
- If the drink is thick enough, add almond milk and blend again.
- Pour it into a glass, and sip.

Spinach as well as Kale Smoothie

The smoothie was created from kale and spinach, each known for its rich nutrients, including minerals and vitamins that are vital for preventing aging.

Ingredients:

- 1/2 cup fresh spinach leaves
- 1/2 cup fresh Kale leaves
- 1/2 cup coconut milk
- 1/2 cup frozen banana
- 1 tablespoon honey
- 1/4 teaspoon vanilla extract

Preparation:

- Blend in a food processor, and mix the leaves of spinach, kale, milk, frozen bananas, vanilla extract, and honey.
- Blend at the highest speed to blend until it is smooth, approximately 30 minutes.
- If the drink is thick enough, you can add more coconut milk and blend it again.
- Pour the drink into a glass and then sip.

Green Tea and Avocado Smoothie

This smoothie is made using green tea, recognized for its high antioxidant content and capacity to fight against the effects of age, and avocado, renowned as a healthy source of fat and power to help collagen production.

Ingredients:

- 1/2 cup of green tea brewed
- 1/2 avocado
- 1/2 cup coconut milk
- 1/2 cup frozen pineapple
- 1 tablespoon honey
- 1/4 teaspoon vanilla extract

Preparation:

- Blend in a blender. Mix the chilled green tea avocado, coconut milk, chilled pineapple, and honey, along with vanilla extract.
- Blend at the highest speed to blend until it is smooth. It should take about 30 minutes.
- If your smoothie seems too thick, add more coconut milk and blend it again.
- Pour it into a glass, and sip.

Bubble tea

BUBBLE TEA RECIPES

The drink sometimes referred to as pearl milk or boba tea, is a well-loved Taiwanese drink made up of milk, tea, and soft tapioca pearls. Here are the 10 best bubble tea recipes that include different fruits to provide additional flavor and nutrients.

Tea Strawberry bubble

The classic bubble tea flavor is made from fresh strawberries and is sweetened with honey.

Ingredients:

- 1 cup fresh strawberries
- 1/4 cup honey
- 1 cup black tea 1 cup black
- 1 cup milk
- 1/4 cup tapioca pearls

Preparation:

- Blender, blend the honey and strawberries.
- Make the tea, then allow it to cool.
- In a pitcher, Mix with tea and milk.
- In a separate saucepan, prepare the pearls of tapioca in accordance with the directions on the packaging.
- After cooking, Add the pearls to the pitcher.
- Shake well, then serve on the ice.

Mango champagne tea

This tropical take to bubble tea is created using fresh mango, then sugar to sweeten it.

Ingredients:

- 1 cup of fresh mango
- 1/4 cup sugar
- 1 cup green tea 1 cup green
- 1 cup milk
- 1/4 cup tapioca pearls

Preparation:

- With a blender, blend both the sugar and mango.
- Green tea, brew, and allow it to cool.
- Make a mix of mango puree with tea and milk in a pitcher.
- In a separate saucepan, prepare the tapioca pearls according to the instructions on the package.
- After the food has been cooked, Add the pearls to the pitcher.
- Shake well, then serve on the ice.

Pineapple bubble tea

This refreshing tea is made using fresh pineapple and is sweetened with sugar.

Ingredients:

- 1 cup fresh pineapple
- 1/4 cup sugar
- 1 cup black tea 1 cup black
- 1 cup milk
- 1/4 cup tapioca pearls

Preparation:

- With a blender, blend your pineapple with sugar.
- The tea is brewed, and allowed to cool.
- In a pitcher, make a mixture of the puree of pineapple, tea, and milk.
- In a separate pan, cook the pearls of tapioca per the directions on the packaging.
- Once the food is cooked Once cooked, add the pearls to the pitcher.
- Shake well, then serve on Ice.

Blueberry Bubble tea

This distinctive bubble tea flavor is made using fresh blueberries and is sweetened with honey.

Ingredients:

- 1 cup fresh blueberries
- 1/4 cup honey
- 1 cup black tea 1 cup black
- 1 cup milk
- 1/4 cup tapioca pearls

Preparation:

- With a blender, blend the honey and blueberries.
- The tea is brewed, and allow it to cool.
- Mix in a pitcher of blueberries with tea and milk.
- In a separate pan, cook the pearls of tapioca according to the instructions on the package.
- After cooking Once cooked, add the pearls to the pitcher.
- Shake well before serving on the ice.

Mango Blend of bubble tea

This smoothie is ideal for people who appreciate mango's delicious and sweet taste. It's also a fantastic method to cool down on the hottest day.

Ingredients:

- 1 cup frozen mango chunks
- 1 cup of milk or non-dairy milk
- 1/4 cup black tapioca pearls
- 2 tablespoons of honey or agave nectar

Preparation:

- Blender: mix the mango chunks frozen and milk or non-dairy milk, as well as honey, honey, or agave nectar. Blend until the mixture is smooth.
- In a small pot, prepare the water to a simmer and add the black pearls of tapioca. The pearls should cook for approximately five minutes or till the pearls become soft and transparent.
- Then drain the pearls from the tapioca, and rinse them in cold water.
- Divide the pearls of tapioca into 2 glasses at the base. Glasses.
- Pour the mango juice over the tapioca pearls inside the glasses.
- Mix well, and then enjoy!

Strawberry Bubble Tea Smoothie

The smoothie contains a tasty mix of sweet strawberries and soft tapioca pearls.

Ingredients:

- 1 Cup frozen strawberry
- 1 cup of milk or non-dairy milk
- 1/4 cup black tapioca pearls
- 2 tablespoons of honey or agave nectar

Preparations:

- With a blender, blend your frozen strawberry, non-dairy or milk, honey, or agave nectar. Blend until it is smooth.
- In a small pot, prepare the water to a boil, then add the black pearls of tapioca. Cook for 5 mins or so until they become soft and transparent.
- Take out the pearls of tapioca and rinse them in cold water.
- Split the pearls of tapioca in one of the two glasses.
- Pour the strawberry drink over the tapioca pearls inside the glasses.
- Mix gently, and then enjoy!

Pineapple bubble tea smoothie

Pearls of tapioca and pineapple are an ideal match in this refreshing tropical smoothie.

Ingredients:

- 1 cup frozen pineapple chunks
- 1 cup of non-dairy or milk milk
- 1/4 cup black tapioca pearls
- 2 tablespoons of honey or agave nectar

Instructions:

- With a blender, mix the chunks of frozen pineapple milk, non-dairy milk, honey, or even agave nectar. Blend until the mixture is smooth.
- In a small pot, prepare the water to a boil, then add the black pearls of tapioca. The pearls should cook for approximately five minutes or till the pearls become soft and transparent.
- Take out the pearls of tapioca and rinse them in cold water.
- Split the pearls of tapioca into 2 glasses at the base. Glasses.
- Pour the smoothie with the pineapple over the tapioca pearls inside the glasses.
- Mix gently, and then enjoy!

Tea Peach Bubble

This blend combines the sweetness of peaches with the rich taste of milk tea, creating refreshing and delicious bubble tea.

Ingredients:

- 1 cup of fresh or frozen peaches
- 1/2 cup black tea or Oolong tea
- 1 cup almond milk
- 2-3 tablespoons honey or sweetener of your choice
- 1/4 cup tapioca pearls

Preparations:

- The tea is brewed and then allowed to cool completely.
- With a blender, mix peaches, tea-brewed almond milk, and sweetener. Blend until it is smooth.
- Cook the pearls in tapioca in accordance with the directions on the packaging.
- Blend the drink in a glass. Then add cooked tapioca pearls, and then enjoy!

Pineapple Coconut Bubble tea

This recipe for tropical-inspired bubble tea is a perfect blend of sweetness and tart flavors of coconut and pineapple.

Ingredients:

- 1 cup of fresh or frozen pineapple
- 1/2 cup coconut milk
- 1/2 cup of black tea that is cursed or Oolong tea
- 2-3 tablespoons honey or sweetener or preference
- 1/4 cup tapioca pearls

Preparations:

- Make the tea, then allow it to cool completely.
- Blends coconut milk, pineapple, and cursed tea and sweetener with a blender. Blend until it is smooth.
- Cook tapioca pearls in accordance with the directions on the packaging.
- Blend the drink in a glass. Sprinkle with the cooked pearls of tapioca and drink it!

Mango champagne tea

This recipe for a smoothie is ideal for the summer months, thanks to the delicious and sweet flavor of ripe mangoes.

Ingredients:

- 1 cup of fresh or frozen mango
- 1/2 cup of black tea that is cursed or Oolong tea
- Half a cup of almond milk
- 2-3 tablespoons of honey or sweetener of preference
- 1/4 cup tapioca pearls

Preparations:

- Make the tea, then allow it to cool completely.
- With a blender, mix mango cursed tea, apricot milk, and sweetener. Blend until the consistency is smooth.
- Cook the pearls in tapioca in accordance with the directions on the packaging.
- Blend the drink in a glass. Then add cooked tapioca pearls, and then enjoy!

CONCLUSION

In the end, the book provides an extensive overview of smoothies and bubble tea's benefits. We've discussed the advantages of including smoothies in your diet and the various types of smoothies, including breakfast and energy drinks and meal replacement smoothies. We also discuss detoxifying and cleansing smoothies, vegan and vegetable smoothies as well as anti-aging smoothies. We also provide an easy-to-follow guide on how to prepare your smoothies. This includes the various bases that could be utilized and suggestions on making and keeping the smoothies.

We also have an assortment of delicious and simple-to-make smoothie recipes that meet various dietary requirements and preferences, such as breakfast smoothies, energy smoothies, and meal replacement smoothies. Cleansing and detoxifying smoothies, vegan and vegetable smoothies, anti-aging drinks along with bubble teas. We hope this book will encourage you to experiment with different ingredients to create your unique smoothie recipes.

Smoothies aren't just delicious and refreshing; they're also an easy and convenient method of incorporating fruits and vegetables into your diet. This will enhance your overall health and overall well-being. Make sure you use top-quality and fresh ingredients and consult your physician before modifying your diet. With this book as a reference that you've read, you're now prepared to prepare healthy and tasty blended drinks and bubble teas at your home. Happy blending!

MEASUREMENT CONVERSION TABLE

Here's a conversion measurement table that can be used throughout the book:

Measurement	Equivalent
1 teaspoon	5 milliliters
1 tablespoon	15 milliliters
1 cup	240 milliliters
1 pint	480 milliliters
1 quart	960 milliliters
1 liter	1000 milliliters
1 ounce	28 grams
1 pound	454 grams

This table can convert measurements for ingredients used in the smoothie recipes provided in the book. It's important to note that these conversions are approximate and may not be exact, so it's always best to use a kitchen scale for more precise measurements.

It's also worth mentioning that the ratio of liquid to frozen ingredients should be adjusted accordingly if you are using frozen fruits or ice cubes.

Printed in Great Britain
by Amazon